SACRED SOLOS FOR B♭ TRUMPET OR B♭ CLARINET

Arranged by Marty Parks

The B♭ trumpet/B♭ clarinet solo folio is only temporarily stapled to the center of the book. It is easily removed by a slight outward pull.

Kansas City, MO 64141

CONTENTS

	Piano	B♭ Trumpet/ B♭ Clarinet
BE EXALTED	5	4a
Be Exalted, O God		
The Heavens Declare		
Be Thou My Vision	51	18a
Do You Know My Jesus?	63	22a
GLORIOUS IS THY NAME	36	14a
Glorious Is Thy Name (Mozart)		
Glorious Is Thy Name (McKinney)		
GOODBY, WORLD, GOODBY	43	16a
Goodby, World, Goodby		
When the Roll Is Called Up Yonder		
In the Presence of Jehovah	25	10a
Just Over in the Gloryland	32	12a
Lord, I Lift Your Name on High	58	20a
My Wonderful Lord	13	6a
OUR GREAT SAVIOR MEDLEY	18	8a
Our Great Savior		
Lord, We Praise You		
Praise God, from Whom All Blessings Flow		
THE HONORS OF THY NAME	68	24a
O for a Thousand Tongues		
Blessed Be the Name		
TRAVELING ON	75	26a
I Feel like Traveling On		
We'll Work Till Jesus Comes		

Be Exalted

Be Exalted, O God
The Heavens Declare

Arranged by Marty Parks

*Music by Brent Chambers.

23
E♭/B♭
B♭
Dm7/A
Gm
Gm/F
C/E
CD: 03
27
F
F/E♭
Dm7
Cm7
F7
B♭
Cm7/4
cresc.
f
f
B♭/D
B♭/C
B♭
F
C7/G
F/A
F
F/E♭
Dm7
6
31
Cm7
Cm9
F2
F
Fsus
E♭/F
B♭
B°7

35
Cm4 7
Cm7
F7
B♭
Cm4 7
B♭/D
B♭
39
F
C7/G
F/A
F
F/E♭
Dm7
6
Cm7
Cm9
F2
F
E♭/F
F
B♭
B♭/A
E♭/G
43
CD: 04
C
C/B
F/A
C2

47
*"The Heavens Declare"
Legato
mp
C2
FM9/C
mp
tr
50
FM9/C
C2
FM9/C
53
G7/C
C2
FM9/C
tr
56
CD: 05
FM9/C
C2
FM9/C

59
G7/C
A♭
B♭2
C2
63
A♭
B♭2
cresc.
C2
mf
A♭
B♭2
mf
cresc.
CD: 06
f
C
C7
A♭
B♭
F sus
f
68
F
Cm7
F7
B♭
Cm4 7
B♭/D
B♭

72
F
C7/G
F/A
F
F/E♭
Dm7
6
Cm7
Cm9
F2
F
Fsus
E♭/F
B♭
B°7
Cm4 7
Cm7
F7
76
B♭
Cm4 7
B♭/D
B♭
F
C7/G
80
F/A
F
F/E♭
Dm7
6
Cm
G/D
Cm/E♭
F
F/E♭

84
B♭/D
D/F♯
Gm
F/G
Gm7
Cm7
Cm9
CD: 07
F2
F
C7sus
C7sus/F
F
B♭
B♭/A
E♭/G
88
B♭
B♭/A
E♭/G
B♭
B♭/A
ff
B♭/A
E♭/G
F
B♭
F7
B♭
G♭
Fm7
B♭
8vb

My Wonderful Lord

CD: 08

HALDOR LILLENAS
Arranged by O.D. Hall, Jr.
Solo arrangement by Marty Parks

With devotion ♩= ca.88

13
E♭
G 7♯5
A♭
CD: 09 1st time
CD: 11 2nd time
17
Fm
A♭m6/C♭
E♭/B♭
3
B♭7
A♭/B♭
B♭7
21
mf-f
E♭
A♭/E♭
E♭
A♭/B♭
B♭13
E♭
E♭M7
E♭7
D♭/F
E♭/G
mf
25
A♭
A♭°
A♭
Fm7
Gm/B♭
Fm/B♭
E♭

Cm
Dm6/C
E♭/C
C7♭9/G
C7
Fm/A♭
B♭7
B♭13
29
E♭
E♭M7
E♭7
D♭/F
E♭7/G
A♭
A♭°
A♭
CD: 10 1st time
CD: 12 2nd time
33
Fm7
A♭m6/C♭
E♭/B♭
E♭°/B♭
E♭/B♭
B♭
A♭/C
B♭
1
D.S.
(to pg. 13, meas. 5)
2
E♭
A♭/B♭
mf
mp
E♭
E♭/D

39
C7sus C7 Bb/D C7/E
F FM7 F7 Gm7 A7#5
43
Bb Bbo Bb Gm7 Am/C Gm/C F
Dm Em6/D F/D D7b9/A D7 Gm/Bb Bb/C C7
47
F FM7 F7 Gm7 A7#5 Bb Bbo Bb

CD: 13
51
Gm
Am
B♭m
F/C
C7
B♭/C
C7
rit.
55
mf
F
rit.
ten.
B♭m6
ten.
F/A
mf
C7/G
F13
F7♯5
59
B♭2
B♭
E♭9
B♭m
F/C
F°/C
F/C
molto rit.
(6)
decresc.
mp
C7
B♭/C
C7
B♭/F
decresc.
F
molto rit.
mp

Our Great Savior Medley

Our Great Savior
Lord, We Praise You
Praise God, from Whom All Blessings Flow

CD: 14

Arranged by O.D. Hall, Jr.
Solo arrangement by Marty Parks

* Music by Rowland H. Prichard. Arr.

CD: 15 1st time

CD: 17 2nd time

30
B♭
E♭/B♭
B♭/A♭
Gm
Gm7
Cm
B°7
E♭/B♭
34
A♭M9
Fm
Cm6/A
B♭
B♭9/A♭
E♭/G
E°7
mf
Fm
Fm7/E♭
D°7
Cm2
Cm7/B♭
Cm/A
B♭
A♭/B♭
B♭/A♭
38
CD: 16
1st time
1
(to pg. 19, meas. 10)
E♭/G
Gm7
A♭
Gm7
Fm7
E♭/B♭
B♭7
E♭
A♭/C
B♭

CD: 18
rit.
decresc.
46 *"Lord, We Praise You"
1st time
2nd time
50

2
CD: 19
rit.
56
*"Praise God, from Whom All Blessings Flow"
A♭
mf
D♭
A♭7/E♭
rit.
D♭2/F
G♭
F7
B♭m
A♭/E♭
E♭7
A♭
G♭/A♭
Fm/A♭
A♭
A♭/G♭
60
D♭/F
Fm7
G♭
A♭2/G♭
D♭/F
E♭m
A♭/E♭
D♭M7
D♭6
65
cresc.
A♭7sus
A♭7
E♭m/G♭
f
F
Fsus/G
F7/A

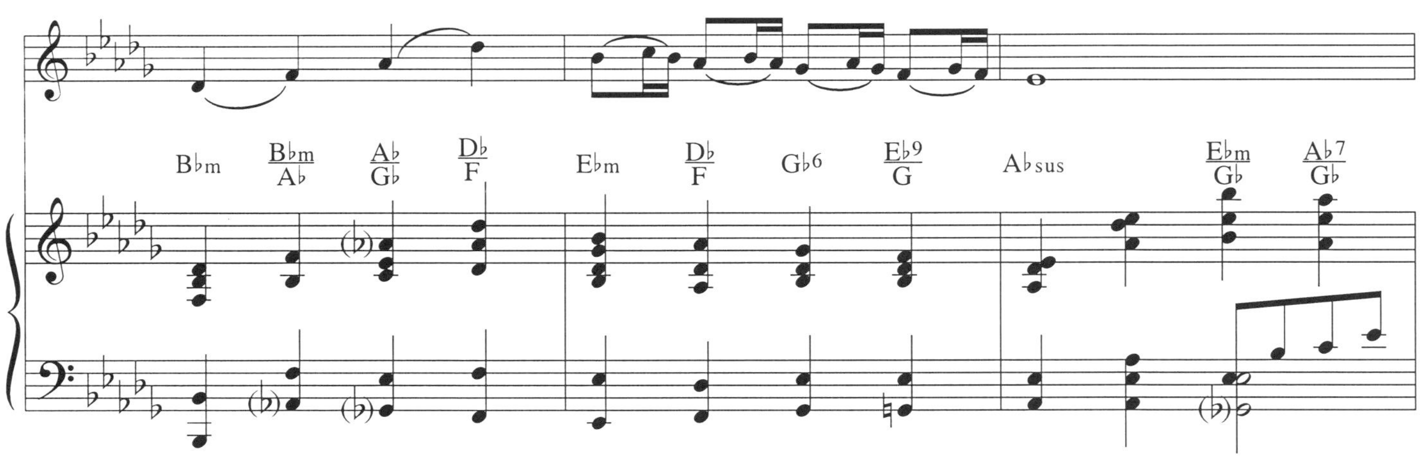
B♭m
B♭m/A♭
A♭/G♭
D♭/F
E♭m
D♭/F
G♭6
E♭9/G
A♭sus
E♭m/G♭
A♭7/G♭

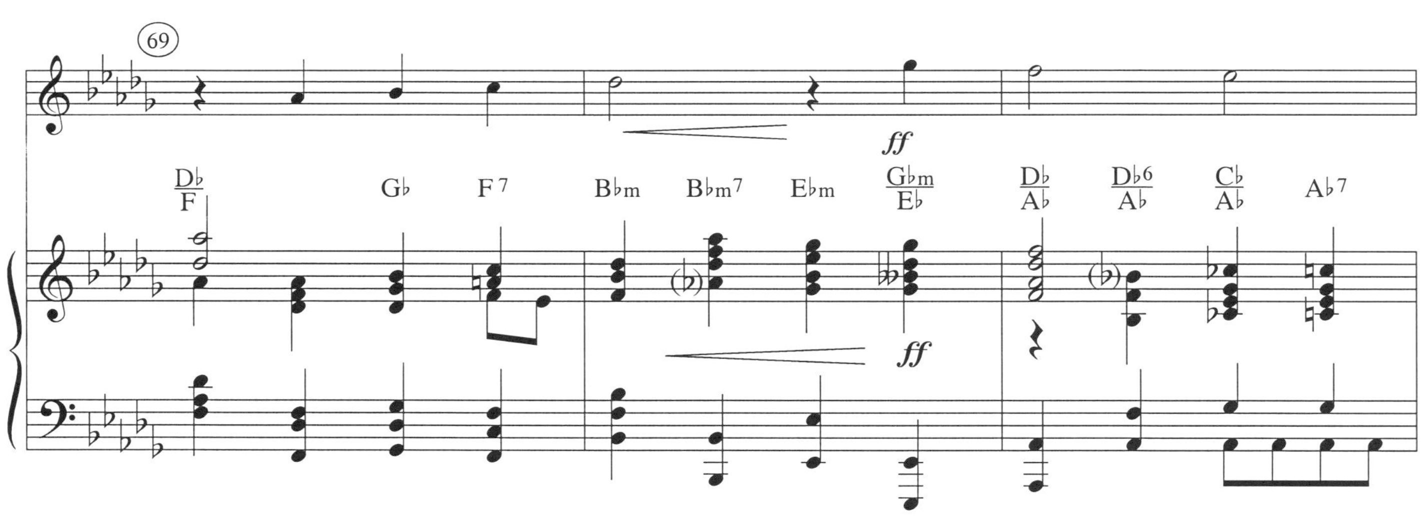
69
ff
D♭/F
G♭
F7
B♭m
B♭m7
E♭m
G♭m/E♭
D♭/A♭
D♭6/A♭
C♭/A♭
A♭7
ff

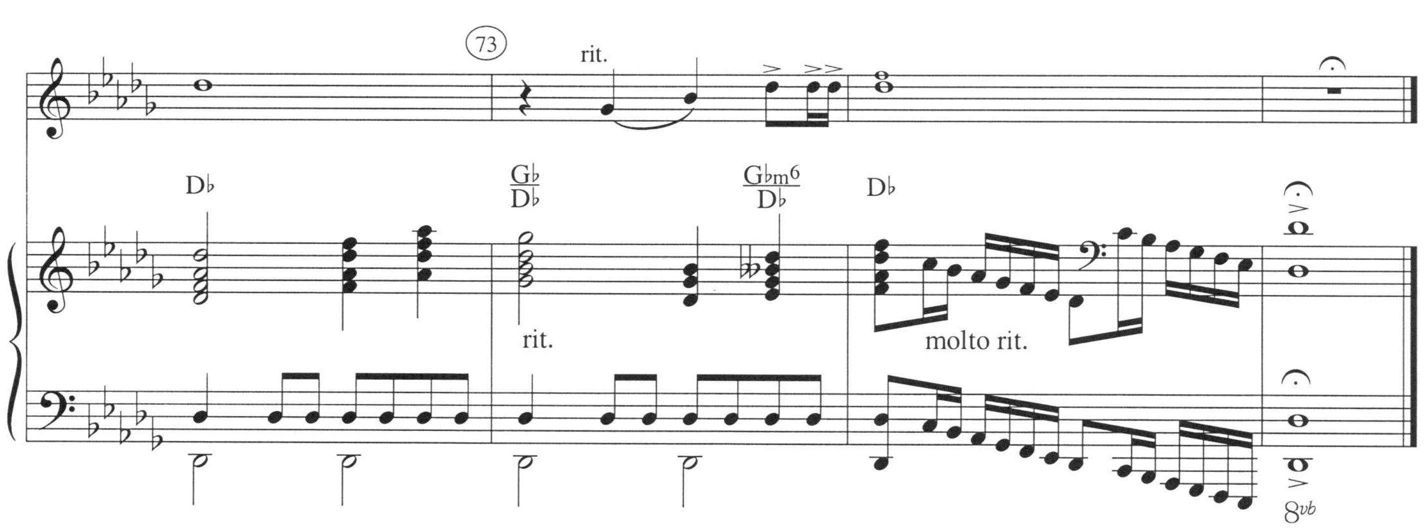
73
rit.
D♭
G♭/D♭
G♭m6/D♭
D♭
rit.
molto rit.
8vb

In the Presence of Jehovah

11
D2 D D/A D D/F♯ G2 G G/D
G Am/F♯ B7/D♯
15
E4 2 Em Em/B G/A A/G
F♯m F♯m7 F♯m7/C♯ Bm7 G/B Bm7
19
Esus E E/B
E D/E E
CD: 21
Em/A Em7/A
rit.
A7
mf
GM7/A Gm6/A
rit.

23
with confidence
a tempo
D2
mf a tempo
F♯m7
27
B7
E4/2
Em
Em7/A
31
D2
GM9
GM7/A
Gm6/A
D2
D2
F♯m7
B7

35
E 4 2
E m
G/A
A 6
D
D/F♯
CD: 22
G M7
D
D/F♯
A sus
mp
41
N.C.
mp
45

49
mf
G
Am/F♯
B7/D♯
E4/2
Em
Em/B
mf
G/A
A/G
F♯m
F♯m7
F♯m7/C♯
Bm7
G/B
Bm7
53
CD: 23
Esus
Esus
E/B
E
D/E
E
cresc.
Em/A
Em7/A
cresc.
rit.
58
Broadly
f
Fm7/B♭
A♭M7/B♭
B♭7♭9
E♭
B♭
f
rit.
Broadly

62
66
70
B♭ E♭
Gm
C9
F4 2
Fm
Fm/B♭
A♭/B♭
B♭6
E♭
Fm2/B♭
Fm/B♭
A♭M7/B♭
B♭7♭9
E♭
B♭
E♭
Gm
C9
F4 2
Fm
F4 2
Fm

CD: 24
B♭
B♭7
E♭2
E♭2
74
A♭
E♭
A♭
E♭
78
slower with freedom
F7
rit.
mp
N.C.
mp
F 4 2
Fm
B♭9
B♭6
rit.
E♭
A♭M7
E♭2
E♭
E♭2
rit.

Just Over in the Gloryland

EMMET S. DEAN
Arranged by O.D. Hall, Jr.
Solo arrangement by Marty Parks

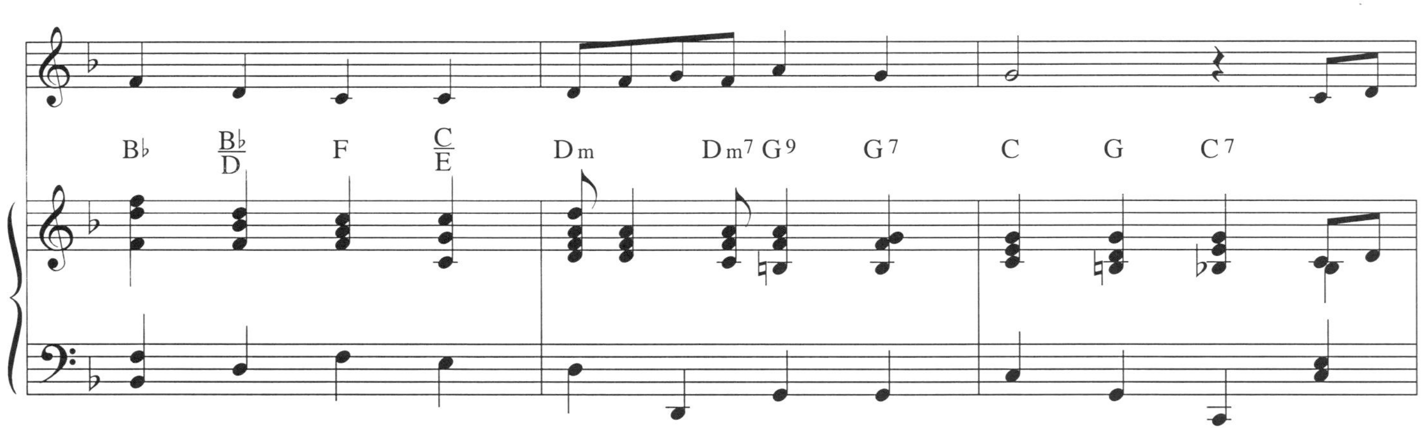

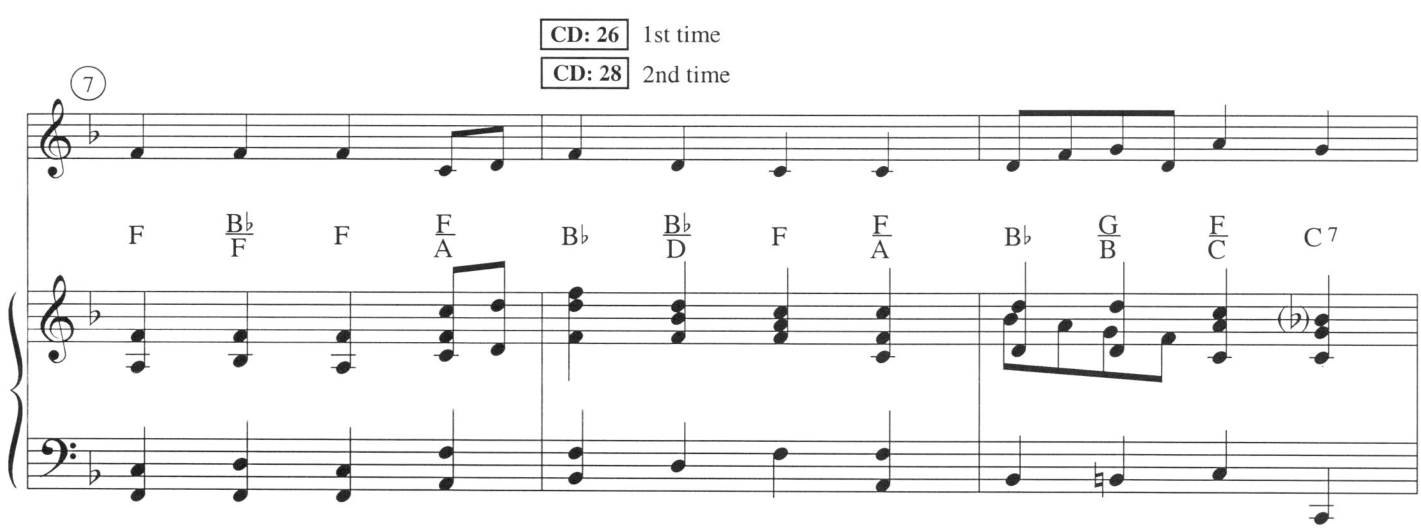

(11)

F B♭/F F C F F6/C F Gm/C F F7

(15)

B♭ B♭sus/F B♭ B♭/D F C/E Dm Dm7/F G9 G7

C G7/D C7/E C F F6/C F Gm/C F F7

(19)

CD: 29 2nd time

B♭ B♭sus/F B♭ B♭/D F F/A B♭ G/B F/C C7

1
CD: 27
(to pg. 32, meas. 1)
2
F
B♭/F
F
F/A
F
F/E♭
D sus
D
Em
F°7
D/F♯
25
G
C/D
G
Am7
A♯°7
G/B
C9
C6/G
C7
C7/E
G
D/F♯
29
Em
Em7/B
A9
A7/E
D
A7/E
D
Em7
F°7
D/F♯
G

CD: 30
1st time
33
G
C/D
G
Am7
A♯°7
G/B
C9
C6/G
C7
C7/E
G
G/B
1
(to pg. 34, meas. 25)
2
C
A/C♯
G/D
D7
G
C2
D
Em7
F°7
D7/F♯
C
A/C♯
G/D
D♯°7
39
tr
mf
f
Em
Em7/D
CM7
G/B
Am7
Am/C
B
B7/D♯
Em
Em7/D
Em/C♯
G/D
mf
f
C
G/B
A
C♯°7
G/D
D7
G
8va

Glorious Is Thy Name

Glorious Is Thy Name (Mozart)
Glorious Is Thy Name (McKinney)

Arranged by Tom Fettke
Solo arrangement by Marty Parks

*Music by Wolfgang A. Mozart. Arr.

10
14
17
20

*Music by B.B. McKinney.

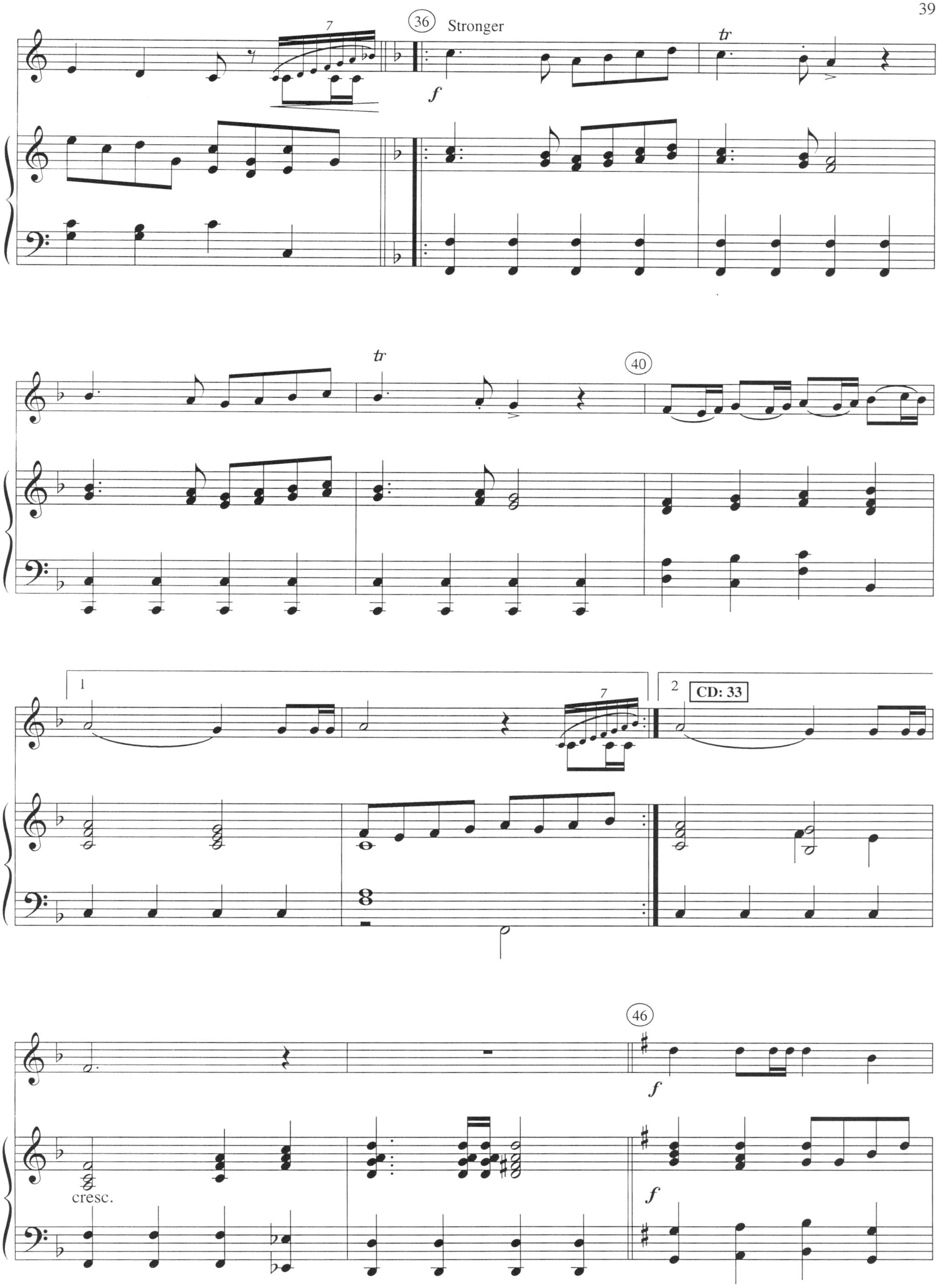

36 Stronger

f

tr

tr

40

1

2 **CD: 33**

cresc.

46

f

f

50

tr
7
54
ff
tr
ff

tr
58

(to pg. 40, meas.54)
1
2
7
62
CD: 34
66
(ff)
(ff)

72
76
80
tr

Goodby, World, Goodby

MOSIE LISTER
Arranged by Camp Kirkland
Solo arrangement by Marty Parks

With energy ♩ = ca. 126

13
E9
D/A
A7
D
G7
D
G6/D
D
G7
D
G6/D
D
17
CD: 36
A7
E+
A7
D
F♯7/C♯
B7
E9
A6
A7
21
D
F♯7

25
B 7
E 7
29
E 7
A 7
E 7
A 7
D
G
G/D
D
G
G/D
D
Em/D
D
33
A
A °7
A 7
D
F♯7/C♯
B 7
E 9
A 7

37
CD: 37
D
Em7
F°7
D/F♯
G
F♯m7
Em7
A
Bm7
C°7
A7/C♯
40
D
G7
D
Em/D
D
G7
D
G/D
D
44
A7
E+
A7
D
F♯7/C♯
B7
E9
48
A7sus
A7
D
G7

3
3
D
G6/D
D
G7
D
G/D
D
52
CD: 38
A7
E+
A7
D
F♯7/C♯
B7
E9
A7
56
D
F♯7
60
B7
E7

E7
A7
E7
A7
B♭7
64
E♭
A♭
A♭/E♭
E♭
A♭
68
CD: 39
A♭/E♭
E♭
Fm/E♭
E♭
B♭
B♭°7
B♭7
E♭
G7/D
C7
72
*"When the Roll is Called Up Yonder"
F7
B♭7
E♭
A♭/E♭
E♭
C7

76
Fm7
D♭9
E♭
E♭sus/F
E♭/G
E♭
E♭sus/F
E♭/G
A♭
A°7
E♭/B♭
82
A♭/B♭
B♭7
N.C.
D
E♭
E
F
B♭
86
B♭/F
F
B♭
B♭/F
F
C
C°7
C7

F
A7/E
D7
G7
C7
91
F
E♭
D♭
E♭
F
E♭
D♭
E♭
F
95
E♭
D♭
Cm7
F
ff
N.C.
E♭
D♭
Cm7
F
ff
N.C.

Be Thou My Vision

Traditional Irish Melody
Arranged by Tom Fettke
Solo arrangement by Marty Parks

14
mp
mp
19
p
p
rit.
a tempo
rit.
a tempo
CD: 41
24
mp

26
3
mp
30
34
mf
mf
decresc.
decresc.

39
mp
mp
42
CD: 42
47
A little faster ♩ = ca. 88
mf
mf
rit.
a little faster
51

55

f

tr

f

60

mf

mf

63

CD: 43

rit. cresc.

rit.
68
a tempo
f
f
a tempo
72
76
cresc.
cresc.
ff
ff

81
rit.
rit.
85
a tempo
a tempo
decresc.
decresc.
rit.
91
Slower ♩ = ca. 76
mp
mf rit.
mp slower
rit.
(6)

Lord, I Lift Your Name On High

RICK FOUNDS
Arranged by Marty Parks

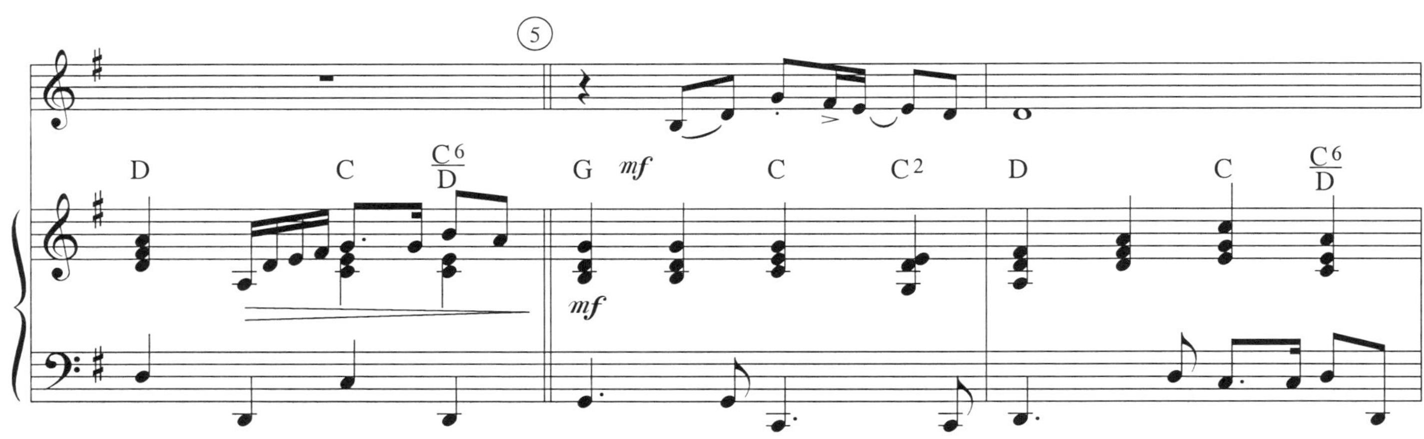

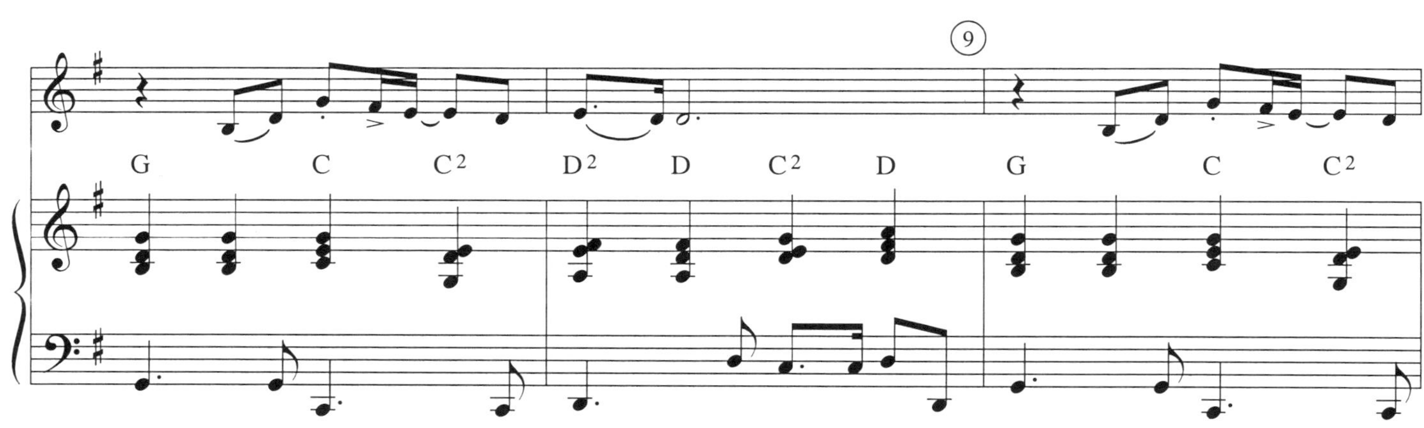

CD: 45
D
C
C6/D
G
C
C2
D2
D
C2/D
D
13
f
G
C6
CM7
D
C
C/D
G
C6
CM7
f
17
D
C
C/D
G
Am7
D
Em7
G/B
CD: 46
C
Dsus
D
G
C
D
C
C6/D

22
mf
G C D C C6/D
mf
G C D C C6/D
26
G C D C C6/D
CD: 47
30
f
G C D2 D C2/D D G C6 CM7
f

D
C
C/D
G
C6
CM7
34
D
C
C/D
G
Am7
D
Em7
G/B
CD: 48
C
Dsus
D
G
C2/G
G
G/F
E♭
D♭/E♭
E♭7
39
ff
A♭
B♭m/A♭
E♭7
tr
D♭
D♭/E♭
A♭/E♭
N.C.
B♭m/A♭
8vb

43
E♭7 D♭ D♭/E♭ A♭/E♭ A♭ B♭m7 E♭ Fm7 A♭/C
8vb
47
D♭ E♭sus E♭ A♭ Fm7 B♭m7 E♭7
CD: 49
A♭ Fm7 B♭m7 E♭ D♭M7/E♭ D♭6/E♭ E♭7
51
A♭ A♭sus A♭ D♭ E♭7 A♭ N.C. A♭

Do You Know My Jesus?

W.F. (Bill) LAKEY
and V.B. (Vep) ELLIS
Arranged by Mosie Lister
Solo arrangement by Marty Parks

13
B♭
C7
F
F7
F9
F7
17
B♭
B♭/D
E♭
21
CD: 51
B♭/F
B♭/D
Cm
B♭/F
F7
B♭
3
mf
25
F7
F9
E♭/B♭
B♭
mf

29
3
F7
F9
B♭
33
B♭
B♭7
B♭9
D
A♭
E♭
E♭
37
CD: 52
B♭
F
F7
B♭
D7
G7
(♭)
3
G7
43
3
C
F
C
C
C7
F

47
F
C
F/C
C
D7
G
51
G7
C
F/C
C
C/E
F
55
CD: 53
F
C/G
G7
G9
G7
C
59
C
f
G7
G9
F/C
f

63
C
G 7
G 9
C
67
3
C
C 7
C 9
E
B♭
F
71
F
C
G
G 7
G♯°7
A m
C
E
D 7
75
mf
rit.
(7)
D 7
C
G
C
E
E♭°7
G
D
D m7
G 7
F
C
C
(♮)
rit.

The Honors of Thy Name

O For a Thousand Tongues
Blessed Be the Name

Arranged by Tom Fettke
Solo arrangement by Marty Parks

With great intensity 𝅗𝅥 = ca.92

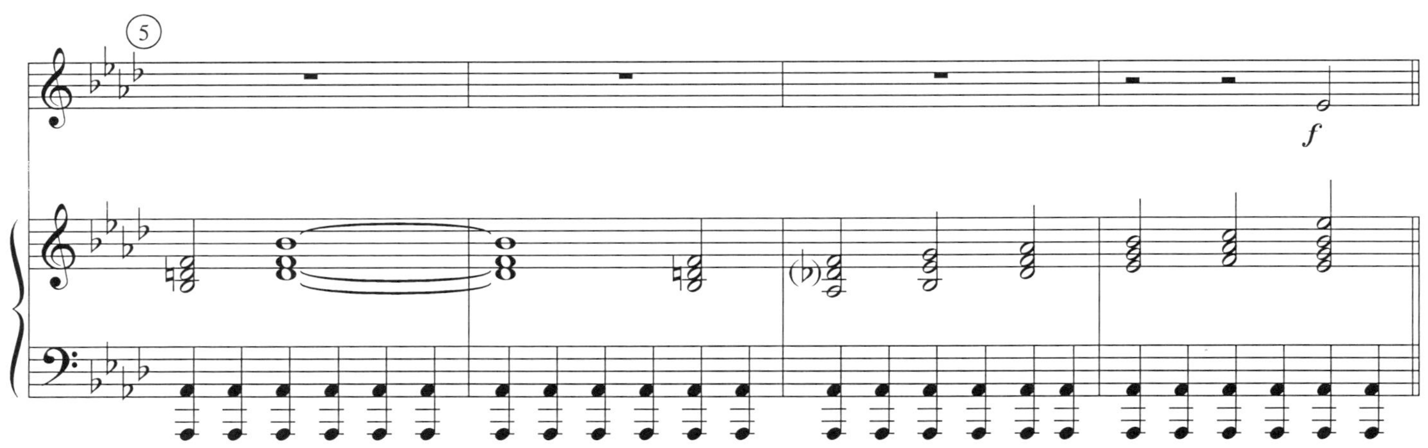

13
rit.
16
Faster ♩= ca. 112
CD: 55
mf
rit.
20
"Blessed Be the Name" (Anonymous)
24

28
32
CD: 56
smoother
mp
decresc.
37
mp

41
cresc.
cresc.
45
f
mf
tr
tr
49
CD: 57
tr

53
57
CD: 58
cresc.
62
f

66
tr
70
rit.
CD: 59
rit.
74
Slower ♩= ca.96
ff
ff

78
sub. mf
sub. mf
82
cresc. poco a poco
cresc. poco a poco
86
ff
ff
great rit.
fff
(6)
great rit.
fff

Traveling On

I Feel Like Traveling On
We'll Work Till Jesus Comes

Arranged by Tom Fettke
and Randy Smith
Solo arrangement by Marty Parks

15
19
CD: 61
24
28

32
36
CD: 62
40
cresc.
42
"We'll Work Till Jesus Comes" (William Miller)
play cued notes 2nd time
f
f

46
1
(to pg. 77, meas. 42)
2
CD: 63
53
55
f
59
CD: 64
2nd time

1
(to pg. 78, meas. 55)
2
64
3
68
cresc. poco a poco
72
ff
ff